Children of the SS Atlantic

The Lives Lost to One of History's Worst Maritime Disasters

Danielle Metcalfe-Chenail

Nimbus Publishing Limited
3660 Strawberry Hill Street, Halifax, NS, B3K 5A9
(902) 455-4286 nimbus.ca

Nimbus Publishing is based in Kjipuktuk, Mi'kma'ki, the traditional territory of the Mi'kmaq People.

Printed and bound in Canada

NB1789

Editor: Penelope Jackson
Editor for the press: Claire Bennet
Design: Bee Stanton
Images of John Hanley and the SS *Atlantic* on the cover are courtesy of Bob Chaulk.

Library and Archives Canada Cataloguing in Publication

Title: Children of the SS Atlantic : the lives lost to one of history's worst maritime disasters / Danielle Metcalfe-Chenail.
Names: Metcalfe-Chenail, Danielle, author.
Series: Compass (Nimbus Publishing)
Description: Series statement: Compass, true stories for kids
Identifiers: Canadiana (print) 20250333260 | Canadiana (ebook) 20250335530 | ISBN 9781774715253 (softcover) | ISBN 9781774715260 (EPUB)
Subjects: LCSH: Atlantic (Ship : 1870-1873)—Juvenile literature. | LCSH: Shipwrecks—Nova Scotia—History—19th century—Juvenile literature. | LCSH: Shipwreck victims—Nova Scotia—History—19th century—Juvenile literature. | LCSH: Nova Scotia—History—1867-—Juvenile literature.
Classification: LCC G530.A84 M48 2026 | DDC j910.9163/44—dc23

Nimbus Publishing acknowledges the financial support for its publishing activities from the Government of Canada, the Canada Council for the Arts, and from the Province of Nova Scotia. We are pleased to work in partnership with the Province of Nova Scotia to develop and promote our creative industries for the benefit of all Nova Scotians.

To the courageous and compassionate

Table of Contents

Author's Note

This true story took place in Mi'kma'ki, the unceded and ancestral territory of the Mi'kmaq or L'nuk—"the people." The Mi'kmaw name for the shore between Prospect and Sambro, Nova Scotia—where the wreck of the SS *Atlantic* took place—is Wetewa'toqsik. It means "noisy place," from the roaring of the sea as it crashes against the jagged rocks of the coast. The Prospect area had been an important part of Mi'kmaw seasonal cycles of fishing and gathering foods and medicines for millennia, and as Mi'kmaw scholar Mercedes Peters says, her ancestors continued to be connected to it even as the **colonial** governments tried to push them out. The Mi'kmaq are absent from this story but not from this time and place.

Another important thing to mention: we don't know exactly what people said to each other the night of the SS *Atlantic* disaster. Some of the dialogue in the pages that follow I found in newspaper articles, letters, and notes taken down in court during the **inquiry** and investigation into the wreck. In other cases, I used my creative license a bit.

Speaking of things that are hard to sort out: The names of rocks and islands around the SS *Atlantic* wreck site have changed over time and depend on who you ask. One island, for example, has been called Golden Rule Rock, Clancy's Island, Marr's, Meaghers, and Mosher Island. My understanding is the locals called it Golden Rule Rock, and so I've generally used this name, but sometimes I've been intentionally vague about the name.

Finally, as far as I know, I am not related to the Henry Metcalfe involved with the SS *Atlantic* story. But family trees can be tangled. Either way, I have tried to be as fair as possible to him and all the other people involved in this harrowing tale.

As you read, look up definitions to the words in **bold** in the glossary at the back of the book (starting on page 79).

Introduction

At approximately 3 A.M. on April 1, 1873, the SS *Atlantic* steamship crashed into the rocky shore of Nova Scotia, Canada. But what became the biggest passenger-ship disaster in the North Atlantic before the *Titanic*—and the worst wreck *ever* in Nova Scotia—has been all but forgotten. This is the case even though victims of the SS *Atlantic* and *Titanic* are buried in nearby cemeteries in Halifax, and both ships belonged to the same company, the White Star Line.

The iron-hulled SS *Atlantic* had left England en route to New York, in the United States. It had successfully made the trip eighteen times before on a regular schedule, and so the nearly one thousand people on board could feel confident they would arrive safely at their destination.

How many people were on board, exactly?

You would think this would be easy to answer, but the historical records don't provide a straightforward number. Add to this the fact that two babies were apparently born on the journey and several **stowaways** snuck on board, and it gets even trickier. SS *Atlantic* historian Bob Chaulk has spent years researching this, and his best estimate is that there were around 950 people on board: 790 passengers (673 adults, 90 children, and 27 infants) and 152 officers and crew. Add 14 stowaways and 2 babies born along the way and we have about 956 people total when the ship was off the shores of Nova Scotia.

The ship had a large crew led by an experienced captain, James Agnew Williams. Most of the crew had also been with the company for some time and sailed on other White Star Line ships—and half had been on the SS *Atlantic* at least once before.

The SS *Atlantic* seemed too big to fail. Standing on the **bridge** of the ship, where the captain and **officers** steered its course, was like being on the fifth floor of a building above street level.

For a week before it sailed, workers piled nearly one thousand tons of coal into the ship's bunkers—enough to fill two big houses. Running out of coal in the middle of the unforgiving North Atlantic could spell disaster: The coal was for cooking and heating as well as powering the engines. The goal was to have just enough on board not to get in trouble, but not so much you were taking up valuable space that paying passengers and **cargo** could use instead.

All aboard!

Besides the captain, the ship had 152 officers and crew, including:

- Chief Officer John Firth
- Second Officer Henry Metcalfe
- Third Officer Cornelius Brady
- Fourth Officer John Brown
- Chief Engineer John Foxley (and 7 engineers)
- a purser, doctor, and the chief steward, with a staff of 40

How big was the ship?

The SS *Atlantic* was 437 feet (133 metres) long, almost 41 feet (12.5 metres) wide, with four steel masts holding twenty different sails. Along with those sails, it had ten coal-fired boilers with twenty furnaces to power the two steam engines. It weighed 3,700 tons. The SS *Atlantic* had seven anchors. The smallest weighed 541 pounds (245 kilograms) and the biggest ten times that (5400 pounds, or 2450 kilograms).

On a good sailing day with the engines and sails full of wind, the SS Atlantic *could go 14* ***knots*** *(nautical miles per hour), or 25 kilometres per hour. With engines only, it still went 13 knots. The trip between England and New York City took ten to twelve days. Today's cruise ships go about 20 knots, and you can make the crossing in seven days.* (BOB CHAULK COLLECTION)

Even with all that coal on board, the White Star Line—like all shipping companies—always prepared for emergencies. The ship carried enough food and fresh water for all the crew and passengers for thirty-two days. But, following the rule of the day, the company calculated the number of lifeboats based on its **tonnage**, not by how many passengers it carried. This meant the SS *Atlantic* carried ten lifeboats, enough for about half the people on board.

There was an able crew and a talented captain aboard a huge ship with the latest technology and a big store of coal. So what was the SS *Atlantic* doing hundreds of kilometres north of its destination of New York? What caused the wreck? How did some people survive? And who was responsible for this terrible tragedy?

Read on to solve the mystery of why the SS *Atlantic* "came to grief," and learn about the children who boarded the ship in England and Ireland, the youngest sailors who worked on it, and the kids in Nova Scotia who tried to help save them all when disaster struck.

Chapter 1

"FULL SAILS AND FULL STEAM AHEAD"

On the sunny morning of March 20, 1873, John Hanley clutched his belongings as he joined the busy docks in Liverpool, England. We don't know for sure, but John was likely between ten and twelve years old, of average height and size for a British boy of the time, with short brown hair parted on the side. He had light skin and blue eyes, and probably wore what other working class boys did at the time: pants, a simple wool shirt, boots, and a cap on his head.

So he wouldn't get lost in the bustling crowds, John stuck close to his parents and older brother, Michael, who was seventeen years old.

Right: John Hanley (sometimes mistakenly written Hindley) was a boy who boarded the SS Atlantic *with his family in Liverpool, England, to start a new life alongside his older sisters in New Jersey, United States.* (BOB CHAULK COLLECTION)

Port officials kept an eye on things as the ship's doctor checked that the passengers were healthy, but even so, fourteen stowaways snuck by them. They blended in with the groups shuttling through the calm waters to the SS *Atlantic,* a huge four-masted steamship anchored in the Mersey River. The smaller boat they used in the harbour, called a tender, had to go back and forth to load roughly 615 passengers preparing to set sail for America, chatting excitedly in English, Welsh, Scots, Irish, German, French, Dutch, Norwegian, and Swedish.

Steamships had been crossing the Atlantic Ocean since the 1840s, bringing millions of people looking to escape poverty or find more opportunities in what Europeans called "The New World," but what Indigenous Peoples had called home for thousands of years. New York City, where the SS *Atlantic* would dock,

Hundreds of people were ferried from the docks in Liverpool, England, aboard a small boat called a tender out to the huge SS Atlantic, *which was docked in deeper water.* (TOM LYNSKEY)

came to be known as the "Golden Door." From there, these new immigrants would spread out across the country to big cities like Chicago. That's where the Cooke family was headed with their grandmother and five children—from George, who was one year old, up to the eldest, Caroline, who was eight. They were from a small town in England called Lewes, where Mr. Cooke worked as a railway porter, carrying bags, cleaning trains, and helping passengers. He only made eighteen shillings per week—less than a hundred dollars in today's money—which could not hope to shelter, feed, and clothe his large family. So they, along with some other local families, were headed to America to make a better life.

Often it was single men or fathers who went ahead to find jobs, get settled, and save up enough money to send for their families. In John Hanley's case, his two older sisters had left years before and found work in the textile mills of Newark, New Jersey, making fabrics like silk, wool, and cotton. Now one was married with children and everyone was excited for their parents and brothers to join them. To pay for the journey, John's parents—like so many others—had likely saved everything they could for years and then sold off their possessions to pay the 6 guineas per person. This would be about $850 Canadian today—a huge amount for people barely scraping by in Britain. Some would convert whatever money was left over from paying for their tickets into gold coins, which they could sew into their clothes, like the lining of a vest. They might wear the vest the whole trip so no one would steal their money.

By 2 P.M., John and all the Liverpool passengers were aboard the SS *Atlantic*, and an hour later it set off for a quick stop in Ireland. The winds were fair, and once they'd cleared the Mersey River the captain ordered the sails set to add speed to their coal-fired journey while the 152 crew members launched into action above and below decks.

The SS *Atlantic* crossed the Irish Sea overnight, and the next morning another 175 people boarded in Queenstown (now called Cobh), Ireland. There were approximately 117 babies, children, and teenagers aboard as passengers, but there were also 6 more young people among the crew: the ship's boys! Sailors were often trained up from a young age to grow into strong adult seafarers. The youngest crew member on the SS *Atlantic* was thirteen years old and on his first voyage aboard the steamship. And Cornelius Lawrence Brady, now a high-ranking third officer, had first gone to sea when he was just nine years old. The ship's boys might run messages between crew, or climb the **masts** to help stow sails, and could stand watch at the **helm** and learn how to steer the ship if the weather was good.

The deck was an exciting place to be on a nice day for passengers too. Kids would play games and run around, even as they struggled to find their sea legs and felt a bit seasick. Maybe John and his teenage brother Michael bundled up against the cold North Atlantic wind and explored after they stashed their belongings in their bunks. They could have stood at the railings and waved to people on shore, scanning the waves for seals, dolphins, and porpoises as seagulls flew overhead. Or the boys might have even flown kites off the back of the ship with the other kids.

In the evening, before the steerage passengers climbed down steep, almost vertical ladders into each of the compartments below and the stewards dimmed the lanterns at 11 P.M., there was also fun to be had. John, Michael, and the other young people on board played cards or dominos, enjoyed the different songs and dances of people from all over Europe, or snuck a peek in the men's area at arm-wrestling competitions and gambling. They also made sure the grown-ups set their watches and clocks back a half hour each night as the ship crossed time zones.

The majority of people on these "emigrant ships" were steerage-class passengers like John Hanley's family. Although the crossing was safer and healthier than it had been years before, it wasn't exactly easy or luxurious for these passengers. John's teenage brother, Michael, slept below decks in the **bow** (or front) of the ship with the single men while John and his parents were in the family quarters near the middle. Steerage-class passengers slept in simple wooden bunks lining the walls of a big open room with hundreds of other people, but at least on the SS *Atlantic* there were toilets so they didn't have to go on the deck when nature called like on other ships.

*When the weather was nice, passengers spent as much time outside on deck as they could. Kids would run and play and even fly kites off the back of the ship! (*KILBURN/LIBRARY OF CONGRESS/PUBLIC DOMAIN*)*

For meals, John and his family would line up with the other passengers three times a day, at 8 A.M., 1 P.M., and 6 P.M. Families had to provide their own plates, bowls, cups, and cutlery, and the meals were all you can eat, almost like the big buffets on cruise ships today. The food was much more repetitive, though. Breakfast was always fresh bread or a biscuit and butter, or oatmeal porridge and molasses. At the

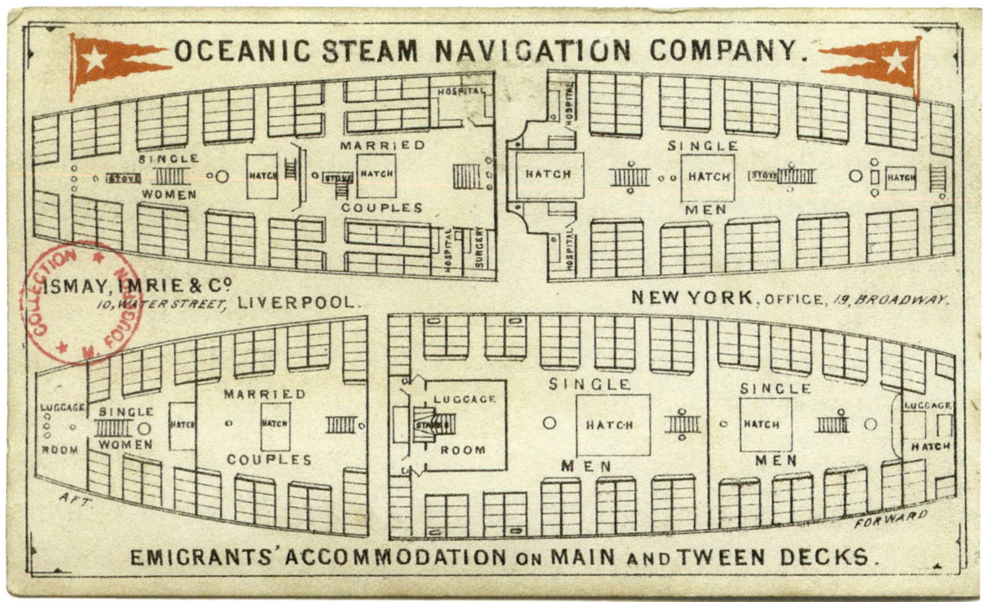

On the lower decks, a thousand steerage-class passengers had bunks in large rooms with small portholes for light and air. The married passengers and families, single men, and single women would all be in separate areas. (CUNARD LINE)

big midday meal, which they called dinner, passengers filled up on soup and salt beef, pork, or fish (depending on the day), bread, and potatoes. Supper, at 6 P.M., was tea, sugar, a biscuit, and butter. At 8 P.M. they might get oatmeal gruel as a bedtime snack, and on Sundays they would get served "pudding," or a dessert. But the food was quite good and plentiful, and most people were thankful for regular meals after tough times at home. They could also bring their own small supplies of food and treats on board in their bags.

There were a few passengers in saloon class, like Lillian Davidson, who was seventeen years old. Her father had died a few years earlier, and she and her mother were travelling to California in the United States to live with Lillian's uncle. Lillian had a cabin that looked like a hotel room, with soft green bedding and an ivory button that rang an electric bell for a steward. This was really exciting at the time—electricity at sea, imagine! She also had access to a bathtub with running hot water heated by the ship's steam engines, and steam piped into the rooms for heating. But no toilet; those were a fair walk away down a corridor. Or, of course, you could reach under the bed for a chamber pot.

The public spaces for Lillian and the saloon-class passengers included their own promenade deck space outside, where stewards delivered snacks and hot drinks. Inside was a huge, beautifully decorated central "saloon" with chandeliers, gold details, fireplaces, a piano, and a library. There were special drinks, including bottles of ginger ale and lemonade for the kids, and big **portholes** and skylights for air and daylight. It looked (and tasted) like the best restaurants in Paris, so of course men would wear tuxedos and women would put on elegant gowns for the evening meal. Of the roughly thirty saloon-class passengers—including two children, a brother and sister—who got to enjoy these perks, many were rich Americans on a trip to Europe for business or pleasure. They were the only ones who could afford it: The cheapest adult saloon-class cabin ticket would have cost about two thousand dollars in today's dollars (although it was half that for kids under twelve, and babies were free).

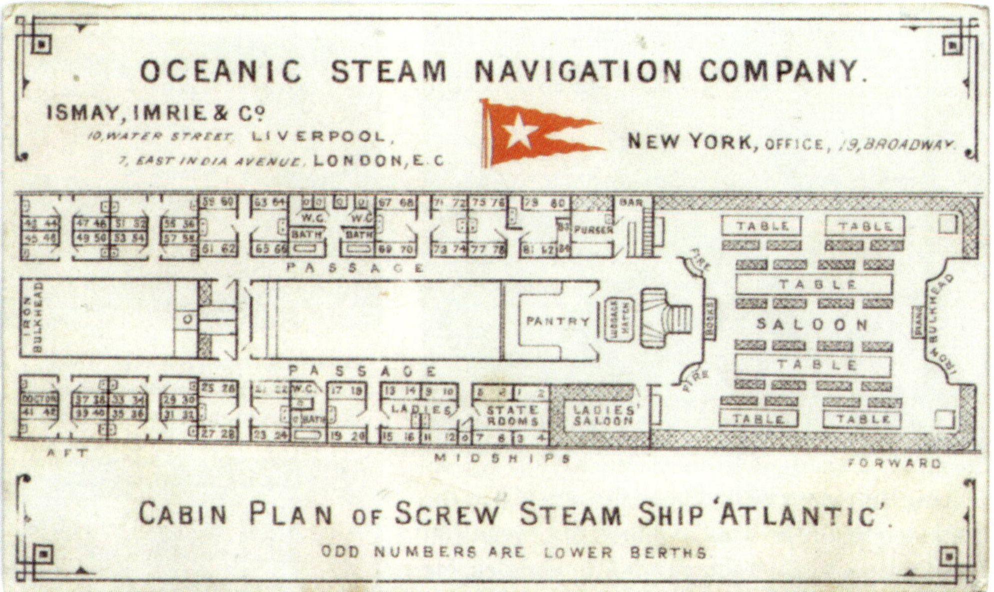

This cabin plan of the SS Atlantic *shows the saloon-class level, where the fancier state rooms could be found and the wealthier passengers enjoyed fine dining and places to relax. (*CUNARD LINE*)*

The first few days brought more good weather, and John Hanley and the other passengers settled into a routine of meals, relaxation, and entertaining themselves by teaching each other words and phrases in different languages. Some mended clothing, wrote letters, or scribbled in their journals. Mothers might comb ever-present lice eggs out of their children's hair with a special comb. A popular activity was tracking the ship's progress on the little souvenir charts handed out by the crew. John and Michael may have watched the captain and crew take sights to calculate the ship's position, trying to guess how far it had travelled.

*Above: Steerage-class passengers spent their time relaxing and chatting on deck when they could, but also sometimes washed their dishes, mended clothes, and did other chores. (*ISTOCK/LUISA VALLON FUMI*)*

*Passengers liked to follow along with the ship's progress at sea, and sometimes made it a game to try to guess how far it had travelled since the last time the crew took the ship's position. (*CUNARD LINE*)*

Then conditions got much rougher. Ships at sea didn't get weather forecasts back then, and the storm seemed to come out of nowhere. The wind whipped up quickly and tore the sails, and the ship rolled and pitched. A lifeboat smashed and some people were even thrown from their bunks. Huge waves crashed down, making it so everyone had to stay below decks except for necessary crew. Those crew members braved ice pellets and sleet to keep a lookout for other ships, icebergs, and even submerged wrecks; below deck they kept watch for the possibility of fire from lanterns and stoves that could be knocked over. The crew also had to close and seal the portholes against the ocean, which meant the air got hot and stinky down below with the noisy heating pipes.

It didn't take long for violent seasickness to set in. Things stayed quite clean in the saloon class, but in steerage they were not so lucky. Water could leak in and soak bedding and belongings, and with only twenty-one toilets below decks for hundreds of people, floors were soon slippery with vomit. The staff served the blandest food possible to settle people's stomachs—if people even attempted to eat—and sleep became almost impossible. Passengers did whatever they could to ease their suffering, but the on-ship doctor couldn't help much. There was only room in the sick bays for eighteen people, and the "medical comforts" he had in stock were lime juice, likely to treat scurvy; mutton broth (a thin soup made from sheep) for coughs and colds; and tapioca, which they might have used to help with diarrhea.

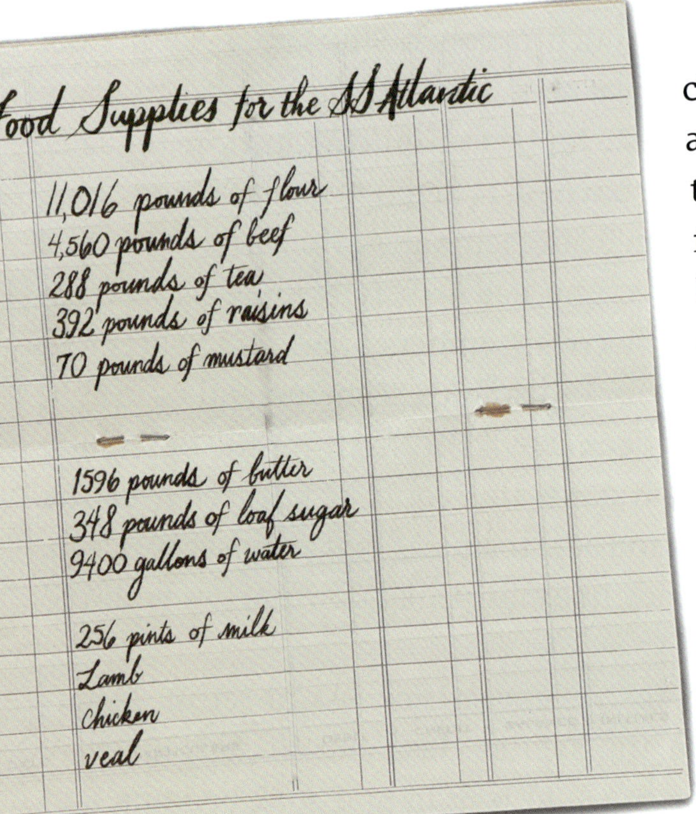
Food Supplies for the SS Atlantic

11,016 pounds of flour
4,560 pounds of beef
288 pounds of tea
392 pounds of raisins
70 pounds of mustard

1596 pounds of butter
348 pounds of loaf sugar
9400 gallons of water

256 pints of milk
Lamb
Chicken
veal

Adding to the chaos, the stowaways on board stole things and caused fights, and two men became obsessed with the idea that the ship would be lost with all aboard. Captain Williams tried to get them to stop scaring the other passengers—and when they wouldn't, he locked them up. People became depressed, bored, and restless, worried the ship might not make it, but the crew reassured them that the SS *Atlantic* was built to handle worse.

The ship's engines devoured coal during the storm. In a four-hour shift the crew used 350 baskets, each weighing fifty to seventy-five pounds. But still, the SS *Atlantic* couldn't keep up its previous speed. This was why, on the seventh day of the storm, Captain Williams wasn't surprised when his chief engineer John Foxley told him they were running low on coal. This kept Captain Williams awake for several nights in a row, worrying.

He finally made the decision to divert to Halifax, Nova Scotia, to refuel.

Ships headed to the United States often went to Halifax if they ran into trouble, so John Hanley and the other passengers weren't too concerned by this turn of events. It would delay their arrival in New York a bit, but at least it meant they would have a break from being on the open ocean, and they would finally see North America, many of them for the first time. Excitement built back up again among the passengers as the SS *Atlantic* powered full steam ahead, the weather cleared, and even a few stars appeared that evening. They had worked so hard for this fresh start, and soon their new lives would begin.

Crew rations

John Davenport was the youngest crew member on board. He was thirteen years old and on his first voyage as a ship's boy. The ship's boys had strict amounts of food, called **rations**, and these were smaller amounts than the adult sailors received. The crew ate regular bread and what was called ship's biscuit or hardtack, which would last for months or even years. The crew had to soak the "cakes" of hardtack in water, tea, or coffee to soften them and make them easier to chew. Sometimes they boiled it and ate it hot with fish and salt pork.

Chapter 2

THE WRECK

When John Hanley and the other nearly eight hundred passengers on board went to bed the evening of March 31, the weather along the Nova Scotia coast was windy and changeable, as it often is in late winter. As usual, lookouts were on duty in the rain and haze to scan the frigid water for boats and other threats. They were also looking for the Sambro Light—the lighthouse on Sambro Island, west of the mouth of Halifax Harbour. It would tell them exactly where the ship was.

Of course, captains need to know where their ship is at all times, but back then they couldn't know exact positions like today. The ships at the time had become more powerful, bigger and faster—and more complex—but were navigated and run using a compass, sextant, chronometer, and what was called "dead reckoning," which was a way of calculating location based on a previous location, speed, how much time had passed, and more. In other words, ship's officers and crew sailed using their intuition, experience, and knowledge passed down from older sailors. The officers might do a quick estimate by the number of revolutions the engine was making, and keep track of their speed using other methods of the day.

Captain Williams would go to the chart room now and then to update the *Atlantic's* position. At midnight, he figured out that the SS *Atlantic* was forty-eight miles (seventy-seven kilometres) from the Sambro Light. But those on board didn't realize the strong west-south-west winds and powerful currents from the Bay of Fundy were speeding them up and pushing them twelve miles (nineteen kilometres) off course. They were actually aiming not at Halifax Harbour but at the Chebucto Peninsula, where the small fishing communities of Upper Prospect, Lower Prospect, and Terence Bay were found.

Captain James Williams was born into a seafaring family in Ireland, went to sea as a teenager, and qualified as an officer in his early twenties. He was already the captain of another smaller passenger liner in the North Atlantic by the age of twenty-six. (BOB CHAULK COLLECTION)

As they approached the Nova Scotia coast, Captain Williams might have told Third Officer Brady what to expect. The lighthouse could be seen about twenty miles (thirty-two kilometres) away under ideal conditions, he shared.

"When you catch sight of the light, wake me. It should be ahead and to port. Then we'll await daylight and fire a blue rocket to call for a harbour pilot to guide us in." Even a seasoned sailor such as Captain Williams would rather wait for daylight to wind their way through all the shoals, rocks, and islands.

As it got dark and the sleepless nights caught up with Captain Williams, though, he decided to take a nap, fully clothed, on a cot in the chart room. First, Captain Williams ordered his steward to bring him a cup of hot cocoa at 2:40 A.M. and wake him.

At midnight, Third Officer Brady handed command of the ship over to Second Officer Metcalfe. "Keep a lookout for loose ice and for the Sambro Light," he said. "When you see it, call the captain. Either way, do not call the captain later than 3 A.M."

At 1:30 A.M. Quartermaster Robert Thomas told Metcalfe it would be a good idea to stop the ship and anchor it offshore. Thomas had been to Halifax Harbour a few years earlier and knew firsthand it was a challenging approach. That's why there were five lighthouses guiding the way into the harbour. "It seemed like a difficult coast to make out," Thomas said later, so much so that he'd told Fourth Officer John Brown "he would not feel the land until he struck on it."

But Metcalfe refused to stop. He stood on the ship's bridge in the dark and biting cold, scanning for the Sambro Island lighthouse as the SS *Atlantic* chugged along at full speed. There were also several other lookouts posted around the ship and there were fifteen crew cleaning the decks and other parts of the ship.

"Can I climb up the main yard to see if I can make out land, sir?" Robert Thomas asked Brown at about 2 A.M.

"No, we're still out to sea," Brown replied. "The ship has not run her distance."

"Sir, begging your pardon, but I think we need to slow the ship," Thomas urged Metcalfe, risking getting in trouble again. "We're getting close to land."

"Remember your place," Metcalfe might have replied, and sent him away. Metcalfe didn't slow down, check the depth, or call on the captain for help. And the captain, at that very moment, had actually briefly woken up, looked around, and gone back to sleep.

The minutes ticked toward 3 A.M. and the wind changed direction to the northwest, lifting the fog and rain. A few stars appeared.

Just before 3 A.M., as instructed, the steward appeared with a steaming cup on a tray.

Metcalfe would not let him pass.

"But the captain wanted me to bring him his cocoa," the steward quietly insisted to his superior officer.

"How dare you challenge me?" Metcalfe retorted, and sent the steward away.

Metcalfe considered calling for the captain at 3:12 A.M. but didn't have the chance. So the captain slept on. And even though the night was clearing, no one spotted the Sambro Light, because they were looking for it ahead and to the left of the boat. But it was directly off to the right.

Instead, the crew saw waves striking granite cliffs.

"Breakers ahead!" shouted a lookout.

Metcalfe ordered the engines reversed and spun the wheel around as Captain Williams ran out of the chart room.

But it was too late.

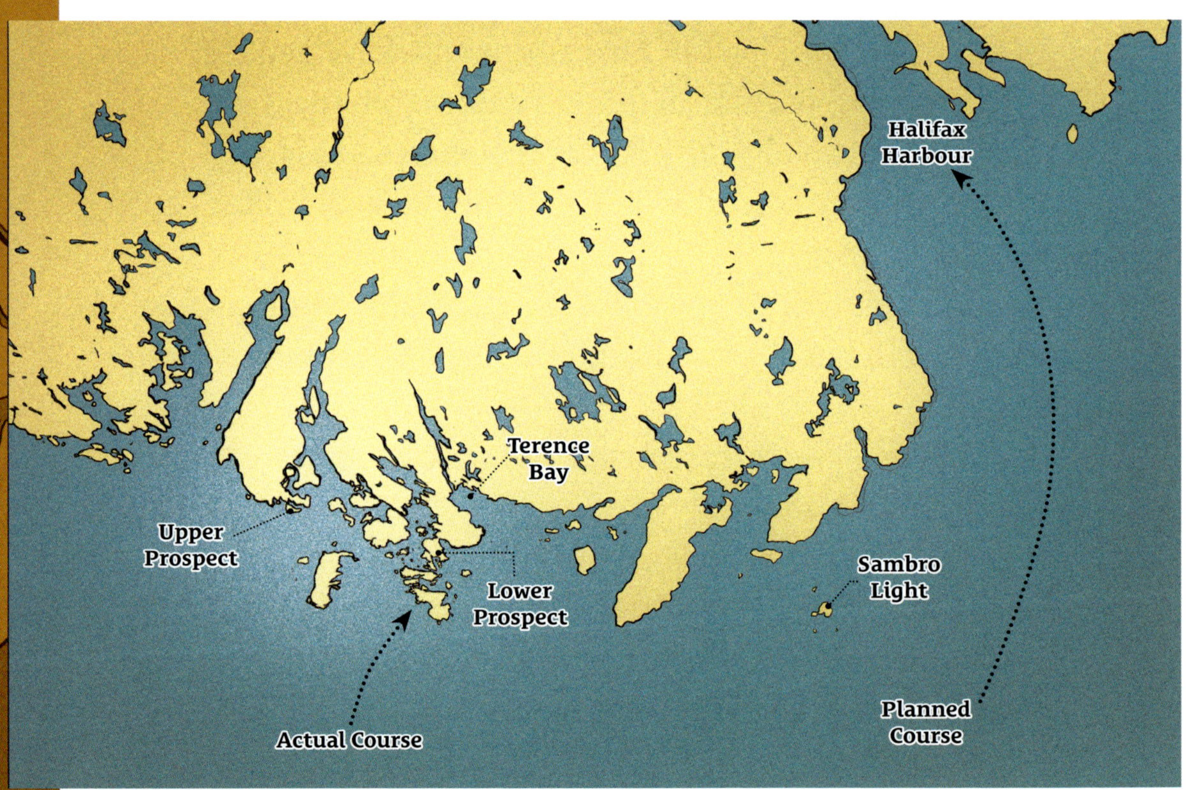

The SS Atlantic*'s route to Nova Scotia.*

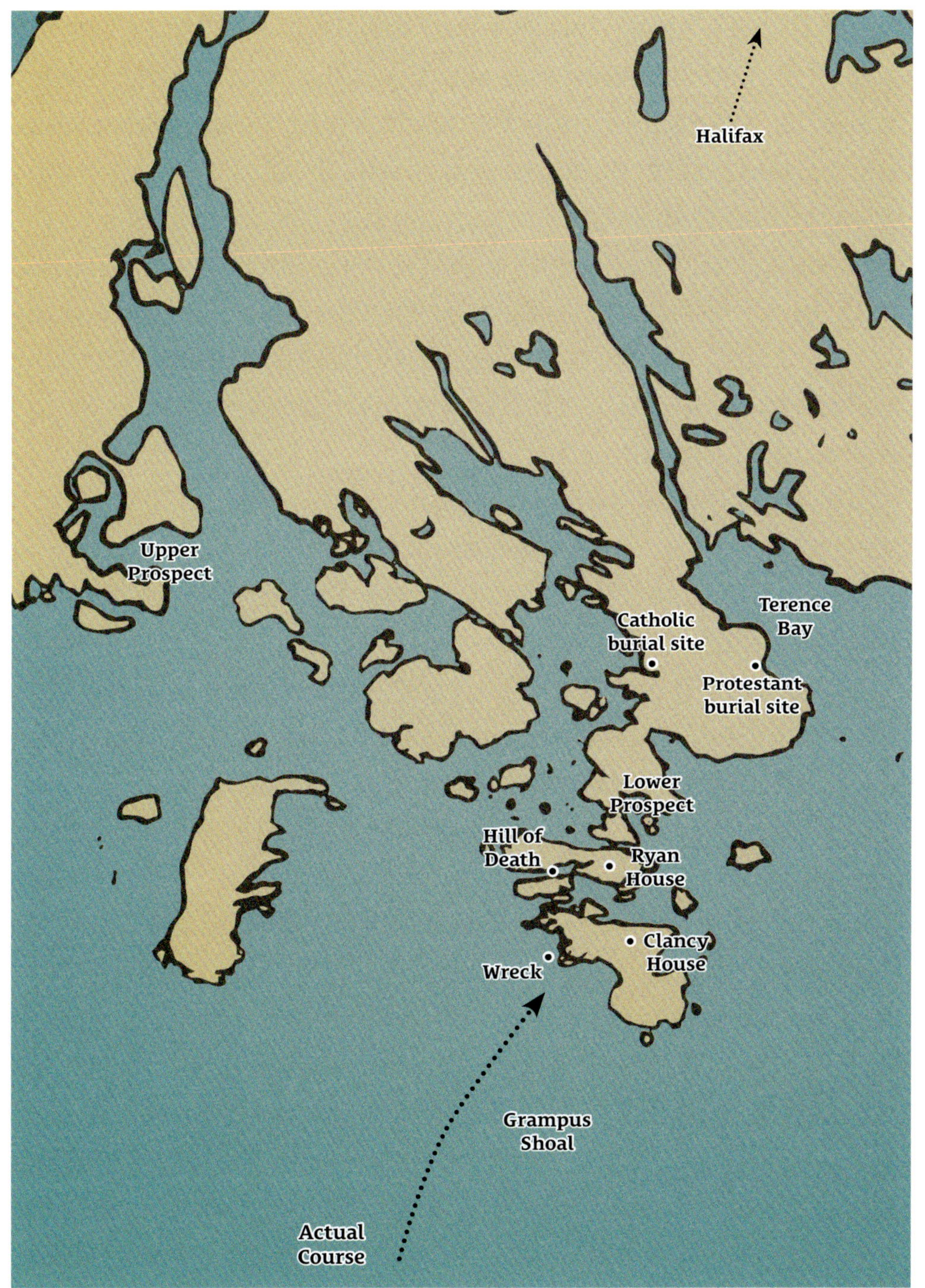
Halifax
Upper Prospect
Catholic burial site
Terence Bay
Protestant burial site
Lower Prospect
Hill of Death
Ryan House
Clancy House
Wreck
Grampus Shoal
Actual Course

The SS *Atlantic* initially plowed into the shallows of the Grampus shoal at full speed, and soon slid up and partially onto Golden Rule Rock, where it slammed to a stop on a ledge. Within minutes the **stern** sank and it began to roll to the left, submerging the rails. Waves swept the deck, dragging crew members into the frigid water. That same water began pouring into the women's and family quarters, where people were shaken from their dreams by the huge crash, most to then sleep for eternity. Those who initially survived tried to claw their way up the narrow stairways to the deck; hardly anyone made it.

Captain Williams awoke and snapped at Metcalfe for his mistake and quickly took in the situation.

"Ready the lifeboats and prepare to abandon ship!" Captain Williams yelled to the officers. But one lifeboat had smashed in the storm, another was destroyed immediately in the wreck, and the others proved impossible to launch. Once the captain realized it was too dangerous, he called the order off, but Metcalfe kept trying. Officer Brady physically prevented people from rushing uncontrolled into the lifeboat, but even so the lifeboat rolled; Metcalfe was never seen again, along with the thirty or forty other men with him.

Below decks, John Hanley and his older brother, Michael, had been sleeping in the bow with the single men, while their parents were in the family quarters. One of the other passengers who was with the boys remembered the moment of impact: "The air rushed in and blew out all the lights, many of the men were stupefied by the shock. It was the impression that the

boiler had bursted." Some guessed the anchors were releasing, and stayed in their bunks, while others like John and Michael apparently changed out of their nightclothes and fumbled their way up the ladder in the dark to find out for themselves what was going on.

But before John and Michael could get topside, the capsizing ship trapped them and the men inside the forward steerage quarters. One man placed John up on a high bunk, where he managed to find a safe spot as the ship rolled.

There was a porthole that was now pointing almost straight up, but the men weren't able to open or break it. How would anyone get out?

The engineers shut down the engines and opened the boiler valves in case the cold water hitting the hot metal made them explode. This added clouds of steam and loud hissing to the terrifying scene. On deck, officers fired distress rockets to signal for help. They streaked across the sky like fireworks.

Then, after about ten minutes, the ship started to roll. It groaned as its **hull** ground against the rocks. Furniture, cargo, and machinery were tossed around inside.

"Take to the **rigging**!" Captain Williams shouted to those who'd made it to the deck.

It was the only way to get away from the rising waters, but as one newspaper later reported, "Walking up the deck of the vessel was as difficult as climbing up the side of a house. Many attempting the task slid off into the sea." Officer Brady managed to get into the mizzen rigging toward the middle of the ship, and as author Greg Cochkanoff wrote, "quickly climbed to the bow, a crossing so perilous that several died trying to follow him." The wind snapped at their bare hands and light clothes as they struggled to grasp the ropes. It was mostly the young, strong men who made it. Passengers who were cold, tired, dressed in long nightgowns, and inexperienced on ships had a hard time managing.

By 4 A.M., about an hour since the SS *Atlantic* had struck shore, there were around four hundred people near the bow of the ship. Many clung to the rigging, not knowing where they were, if help was coming, or if they could survive much longer. Captain Williams apparently did his best to help them, getting everyone to keep moving, flap their arms, and avoid falling asleep as they fought off hypothermia.

No one knew how the ship would move. It could break apart or roll over more, killing all the survivors. With the bow on the rock and the stern on the bottom, there was a lot of stress on the midships section. Add to that the huge weight of the boilers, engines, cargo, **ballast**, and other heavy machinery in the centre of the ship. The hull could snap, the cables supporting the masts could spring at any time, and the steel mast could rush to the bottom and take them down with it.

The captain and others onboard knew they were close to land, but it was still dark, and the water was close to freezing. Some decided to swim to shore and tried putting on the ship's cork lifebuoys, but did so incorrectly and ended up drowning. Others found themselves in the punishing waves, thrown against the granite boulders over and over again.

Even so, they knew that swimming might be their only chance. The captain ordered his officers to get a rope to the rock the SS *Atlantic* had struck. Quartermaster Edward Owens put on a life jacket and tied a rope around his waist. He jumped in and swam, but was overwhelmed with exhaustion and cold, so they pulled him back. Quartermaster John Speakman tried next and actually made it, discovering an unconscious crewman already on the rock. Speakman kicked the man to wake him up and together they secured the rope that had been tied around his waist and hauled Third Officer Brady over.

After about two hours, people realized there were passengers like John and Michael trapped inside the half-submerged forward steerage compartment. They found something heavy enough to smash the glass of a porthole and men began to emerge from the hole. John watched as about six or seven men climbed up and out, but he was unable to reach the hole. The men gave him a boost while another passenger topside grabbed him first by the hair and then by the arm and heaved him up onto the side of the wreck. John then made his way to the bow and joined those huddling there. Michael was not with him.

For an hour or more, John Hanley stayed with the others, all the while being drenched by freezing sea spray, and watching men attempt to cross to the rock using the ropes. Unable to find his older brother or either of his parents, he began to cry. His bunk neighbour tried his best to comfort him.

Before John Hanley had to decide whether he would cross by one of the ropes to Golden Rule Rock, he and the others saw that it wasn't the temporary refuge they'd hoped for: The rising tide was clawing back the size of the rock as it got more crowded, and it seemed impossible to get from there to the shore. It was too far, too cold, and too treacherous.

But the ship was creaking and moaning in the wind and waves, and could break apart at any moment. And people were starting to succumb to hypothermia around him.

How would John—or anyone—survive this wreck?

An artist at the time tried to capture John Hanley's miraculous escape onto the deck through a porthole. (BOB CHAULK COLLECTION / FRANK LESLIE)

Chapter 3

THE RESCUE

Luckily for the people stranded on the rock and in the SS *Atlantic*'s rigging, several fishing families lived nearby. This part of the Chebucto Peninsula was, and is, generally known as Prospect. There were three main settlements at the time which still exist today: Terence Bay, Lower Prospect, and Upper Prospect.

Closest to the wreck site was Lower Prospect, where Michael Clancy and his family had a small home. The sound of the huge ship crashing into the rock actually woke Michael Clancy, and he looked out the window in time to spot the distress rockets. He quickly got dressed and ran out into the icy wind to see what was going on. Then he alerted his brother and son, and the three of them grabbed lanterns before clambering over boulders through thick brush and snow toward the sound. Before long, a shape appeared in front of them: a shivering, soaked Quartermaster Robert Thomas, who had just swum to shore from the ship.

They brought Thomas home and into the care of Michael Clancy's daughter, twenty-eight-year-old Sarah Jane O'Reilly, who gave the survivor dry clothes and put him next to the warm stove. By that time all twelve people in the small house, including Sarah Jane's two young children, were awake.

"Go over to Ryans Island and get Ed Ryan to come," Michael Clancy said to young Eddie Mullins, a relative who was staying with them. Eddie went out into the cold, found his little **dory** nearby, and rowed alone in the darkness around the point, across the cove.

The way in was a small target in the darkness, but Eddie, like all the children of the area, had saltwater in his veins, and by looking at the shapes of the land he made his way along. He was descended from generations of seamen and learned to row a dory the way kids today learn to ride a bicycle. The tips of Eddie's oars touched bottom a few times and he sensed that Norris Island was on his left. He eased the boat to the right, through the channel and into the deep water of Norris Gut. Straight across and the stem of the dory bumped Edmund Ryan's wharf. He whipped a reef knot to tether the boat to the wharf, scrambled up the path to the house, and pounded on the door.

Edmund Ryan was already up, trying to make sense of what he had just heard. He threw the door open and there was Eddie.

"What's going on?" Edmund asked.

"Mr. Ryan, you gotta come! There's a big ship ashore," Eddie replied, out of breath.

Ryan wasted no time. He primed a **musket** and fired a couple of shots into the air to alert people on the mainland that there was an emergency. That drew others from Lower Prospect. Soon, they were all at Clancy's wharf, leaping from their boats. They rushed toward the steam and the noise and soon saw the staggering devastation of the SS *Atlantic*. It was the biggest ship they had ever seen, half sunk, swamped by huge waves. They were overwhelmed at the sight of hundreds of people clinging to life up in the rigging that they knew could spring loose at any moment and plunge them to certain death. Others had managed to pull themselves along ropes strung between the ship and a rock, but the men knew the rock would soon be underwater when the tide rose. And, all around, there were bodies of people they could no longer help. They were shocked, stunned, with no idea where to start.

Photography was very rare in 1873, so most of the images of the ship and the wreck were sketched by artists and published in newspapers and magazines. (BOB CHAULK COLLECTION)

Meanwhile, on the ship, survivors had seen Michael Clancy's lantern earlier and felt hopeful for the first time since the wreck; when it left, along with the group of men, they worried they were being abandoned. Soon, though, a dog appeared on the shore, and reignited their hope. They'd been hanging on for dear life for almost three hours, afraid the ship might break apart below them and toss them into the unforgiving sea. Rosa Bateman, the last woman alive on the ship, was up in the rigging. She sang hymns and led the men in prayers to keep their spirits up in the dark hours before dawn.

Eddie Mullins and other fishermen arrived on the site in their boat about 4:30 A.M. Third Officer Cornelius Brady had managed to swim to shore from the rock; he shared the name of the ship and owners and passed a note in the White Star Line's private company code. A courier on horseback struggled in the foot of snow on the ground to take the note to Halifax so a telegram could be sent to the company's office in New York. At the same time, the other men hurried to wake more fishing families and tell them to come with their boats. To keep up their spirits, Brady painted a sign and held it up high in the dawning light: "Boats coming."

And they were, slowly but surely.

Michael Clancy had his dory in the water, and he, Edmund Ryan, and Officer Brady hiked back to the Clancy wharf and dragged the dory through the woods and over the rocks to the water. But almost immediately the dory began taking on water. They quickly realized they needed something bigger to handle the waves.

Luckily James Coolen had taken his larger **seine** boat out of storage early for the year, and he and some other men arrived at the Clancy wharf from Lower Prospect. But that was across the island and it would take too long and be too hard to go all the way around to the wreck site. The boat needed a dozen or more men to carry it, and while the fishermen were strong, there weren't many of them. So Officer Brady and some of the survivors helped haul it over the challenging terrain, shouldering eighty to a hundred pounds each while trying not to slip or break a leg on the boulder-strewn path. Then they eased it into the sea, getting sprayed by the icy water in the process. Soon Michael Clancy and a crew of men carried his seine boat over the island to join the rescue effort. They pressed Edmund Ryan's seine boat into service as well—carried over the island like the other two before. The boats would be leaky after being out of the water all winter, but it was the best they had. Someone would just have to constantly bail.

Some of these experienced seamen were worried about facing the waves. On the first trip, at about 6 A.M., James Coolen and Dennis Ryan went alone through the rough surf to the rock, and brought the first survivors to shore. That inspired the others to be brave—and the rescue was on, as fishermen took turns going back and forth, fuelled by adrenaline, a sense of duty, and that "Golden Rule" they heard about in church on Sunday, that we should treat others the way we'd like to be treated.

At roughly 8 A.M. Nicholas P. Christian arrived at the wreck site

This photo was taken in 1906 in Upper Prospect, Nova Scotia. It shows a seine boat like the ones used in the rescue of the SS Atlantic *survivors. At least one of the people pictured, twelve-year-old Richard Duggan (in front), was related to the rescuers, in fact!* (MICHAEL DUGGAN)

by sea with others from Upper Prospect. On one of the boats was nine-year-old Tom Hamm of Upper Prospect, who was expected to help with the work. Many of the new rescuers had relatives in Lower Prospect and had spotted the drama unfolding across the water using a telescope. With this fresh energy, the group of fishermen made about eighteen trips to the rock over the next hour and a half to save more survivors. They were working as quickly as they could, but the water kept rising and would soon submerge the rock.

Captain Williams was still directing the rescue from the ship, leaning on his cane, in pain from old injuries. He blocked desperate people trying to butt in line to be rescued. Even so, one time they swarmed a boat as fourteen survivors clambered aboard instead of the usual eight to ten. They were lucky they didn't capsize.

After that near-catastrophe, Williams told the fishermen not to come right up to the wreck but instead to toss a rope, and then whoever caught it on the ship would have to jump into the water and get picked up. While it sounded dangerous, not a single person was lost using this method.

The rescuers also strung lines from the shore to the ship to steady the boats and streamline the process. Survivors arrived by boat on shore every ten minutes or so, hauled out by men waist-deep in the freezing water. It was exhausting work in the boats and they swapped places regularly, but when they took a break, they felt the cold overtake them. The frostbitten survivors even pried shoes, jackets, and shirts from the dead and dried the clothing by the fire so they could wear them.

In this chaos, the fishermen were understandably worried about losing their own lives trying to rescue others. Some kept their boats away from the ship, assessing the situation, and Captain Williams and Chief Officer John Firth made desperate promises of cash rewards. Witnesses heard Captain Williams yell from the rigging to Dennis Ryan that he would pay $500 (or possibly British pounds—the records aren't clear) for every boatload of survivors. "That was an astounding amount of money for the time," historian Bob Chaulk notes, "and it is surprising that they took him at his word." It would be $10,000 in today's dollars.

At some point that morning, men on board the SS *Atlantic* passed John Hanley down to a boat, where the fishermen grabbed him and rowed to shore. John Hanley was likely taken, along with so many, to Michael Clancy's house, where his daughters kept the stove hot, boiled water for buckets of tea sweetened with molasses, and tried to find dry clothing for the survivors. Bob Chaulk notes the helpers fed the survivors with "whatever dried fish, potatoes, salt pork, and beans that remained after the long winter, all spread out on oil-clothed tables." Soon holes had to be drilled in the floor to drain the water coming off the sopping wet survivors. After a quick check, those who were healthy enough moved to nearby homes while the worst cases were put to bed.

By 9:40 A.M. the tide was high and the rock was swamped by water—but they had managed to snatch the last man off it just in time. They'd also managed to rescue everyone on the bow of the wreck. But there were still about two dozen people left on the ship, including Captain Williams.

Finally, the other passengers were rescued and Captain Williams was carried off and placed in a boat; Officer Brady and several others had to hold him up to get him out and onto shore, he was so injured and exhausted. Two survivors remained in the rigging of the SS *Atlantic*, though: Chief Officer John Firth and a seventeen-year-old crewman called Charles Flanly. Even though a large American schooner was anchored in the bay, it could not come near. Smaller boats tried to get to them as well but it was impossible. The tide was too high.

“Hold on!” someone might have yelled. “When the tide falls and the wind dies down, we’ll come back!”

But Firth and Flanly saw the rescuers pull their boats up on shore and felt left behind. James Coolen went home to change into dry clothes and resume the rescue effort, and the fishermen lit fires to warm anybody left on the beach. Watching this, Flanly and Firth felt even colder, lonelier, and more exhausted.

Even so, Firth kept waving and yelling for help.

It was about this time—at roughly noon—that Rev. William Ancient arrived on the scene and thought the fishermen had given up. He rushed to take charge to save Firth and Flanly. Rev. Ancient was in his late twenties or early thirties, ex–Royal Navy and from England. He recruited local fishermen Samuel White, James Power, Patrick Duggan, and John Slaunwhite, and they carefully rowed toward the ship, yelling to Flanly and Firth to go where the boat could pick them up.

But that was out of the question. With their strength and hope nearly gone, and salvation so close, Flanly jumped in. Ancient grabbed him, and pulled him into the boat. They rowed Flanly back to shore before turning back to the ship.

“Jump, man! It’s the only way!” Rev. Ancient yelled to Firth.

“But I can’t swim,” Firth replied.

So Rev. Ancient stepped on the SS *Atlantic*, climbed the steep side to the rail, and secured two long pieces of rope. He tied himself to the wreck in case a wave washed him off, and then put the other over his shoulder. He climbed along to Firth, tying the rope at intervals along the length of the ship, then threw the rope to Firth. The exhausted man tied it around himself, but as soon as Firth moved, his legs gave out and he tumbled into the water, screaming that his legs were broken.

"Never mind your shins, man," Rev. Ancient yelled. "It's your life we're after!"

Then Rev. Ancient hauled Firth out of the water and to the bow of the SS *Atlantic*, where the rescue boat could reach them.

The last survivor was off the SS *Atlantic,* but the ordeal was nowhere near over.

Chapter 4

SURVIVORS AND VICTIMS

Chief Officer John Firth, like all the other survivors, made his first stop at Michael Clancy's house, but there was no room, so Clancy's daughter Sarah Jane had to send the exhausted and injured man on yet another boat ride to Edmund Ryan's house. He, along with the four hundred or so other survivors, went to the roughly ninety homes in the area. Many of those homes were crammed with a dozen survivors recovering from the disaster. These families did what they could, but when the SS *Atlantic* wrecked near their communities, it was the end of March, when supplies were low.

The thin soil in Prospect was not good for growing more than hay for the animals and potatoes for the people. In the fall they would harvest what they could and stock up on things to get them through the winter. Bob Chaulk writes that by April 1 "many would have been living on bread, molasses, salt pork, and tea, and their growing sons and daughters often left the table hungry." They had small homes with big families, and often children were three or four to a bed, "which they didn't mind because it provided company in the absolute darkness, and warmth in the freezing house. There was no electricity or running water or indoor plumbing. Everyone went to bed early to avoid wasting candles or the fish oil that fueled the lamps." The only heat came from a low stove in the kitchen or a fireplace fuelled by coal or wood. In the morning at that time of year, there might still be frost on the floor and a thin layer of ice on the water barrel.

With the families so stretched, and the importance of getting help and word back to the White Star Line so great, Third Officer Cornelius Brady decided to leave on foot to walk the roughly eight hours to Halifax on April 1. Simon Harrie of Terence Bay volunteered to lead him. They left about 1 P.M. in snow that was a foot deep in some places. A little later, about a dozen more followed, including some of the engineers and a few passengers. They rested near Hatchet Lake at Strawhouse, a place well known to travellers, where St. Timothy's Church stands today. Some spent the night there or perhaps in the nearby locales of Brookside or Goodwood, totally exhausted, while others continued to Halifax. They finally arrived about 10:30 P.M. and went to see the mayor, who then directed them to the police station for help. From there,

This is the earliest known photo of the wreck of the SS Atlantic. *About fourteen hours after the ship ran aground, the bow broke off from the ship, and it finished rolling over and sank. Here you can just see the bow broken off in the surf.* (BOB CHAULK COLLECTION)

Brady quickly sent a telegram to the White Star Line's New York agent, who sent an overseas telegram to England—where the *Times* newspaper in London got wind of the story.

It didn't take long for word to spread on both sides of the Atlantic Ocean. Officials in Halifax readied two steamships (the SS *Delta* and *Lady Head*) overnight along with a tugboat. They stocked the boats with food, clothing, and other essentials, and left the harbour at 3 A.M. in order to arrive in Prospect at dawn on April 2. This would give them as much daylight as possible for the work ahead.

When the steamships arrived, they saw wreckage, cargo, and bodies everywhere in the water and on the shore. Boats of all shapes and sizes cluttered the scene as people from up and down the coast had come to help, gawk, or scavenge souvenirs from the wreck. Captain Williams posted crew members to stand watch against pilfering and fishermen from the area also apparently stood guard over bodies, protecting those in death they could not save in life.

The three Halifax steamships anchored offshore and sent a smaller boat in with customs officials to oversee things. Local boats also rowed or sailed their groups of survivors to the bigger ships. There were hundreds of men, most of them in their early twenties. Not a single woman or child had survived except for John Hanley, who had luckily been bunking with his brother in the men's quarters. The men were bruised and exhausted, many of them with frostbite and some with broken bones. The survivors wore whatever clothes their rescuers could spare or even that they had taken from the dead in desperation, along with bits of carpet and blankets.

Two agents stood at the entrance to the SS *Delta* steamship recording names and nationalities as the men trudged up the gangway. No one knew then exactly who was on board the SS *Atlantic*, and to this day the information is unclear: A few babies were born on the trip, stowaways hid themselves aboard, and official letters, reports, and inquiries contained different numbers. Newspapers spelled names differently, and passenger records were lost. Bob Chaulk says in his years of researching the story, he's come up with more than 25 totals of passengers on board. His conclusion is there were around 950 on board and 550 deaths, leaving approximately 400 survivors.

By about noon those survivors who could travel were aboard the ships bound for Halifax. They disembarked mid-afternoon at Cunard's Wharf and citizens of the small coastal city watched as survivors slowly walked down the gangway, past coffins being built for the victims of the wreck. The Cunard company and **Haligonians** generally welcomed people in various languages, guiding them to accommodations, and giving them food and clothes. Cunard officials also helped get letters to loved ones and found them space on steamships to their destinations in the US.

John Hanley got off the ship wearing ill-fitting clothes, but at least he had enough to protect him from the elements. John was the only child to survive the wreck and was now an orphan, so he became the focus of the generosity of the people of Halifax.

Not long after the tragedy, the song "The Little Commodore" was created by Americans Samuel N. Mitchell and George Dana about John Hanley, the only child to survive. "The bravest of the brave was he / That little Commodore," goes the chorus, "And all should welcome heartily / His presence on our shore."

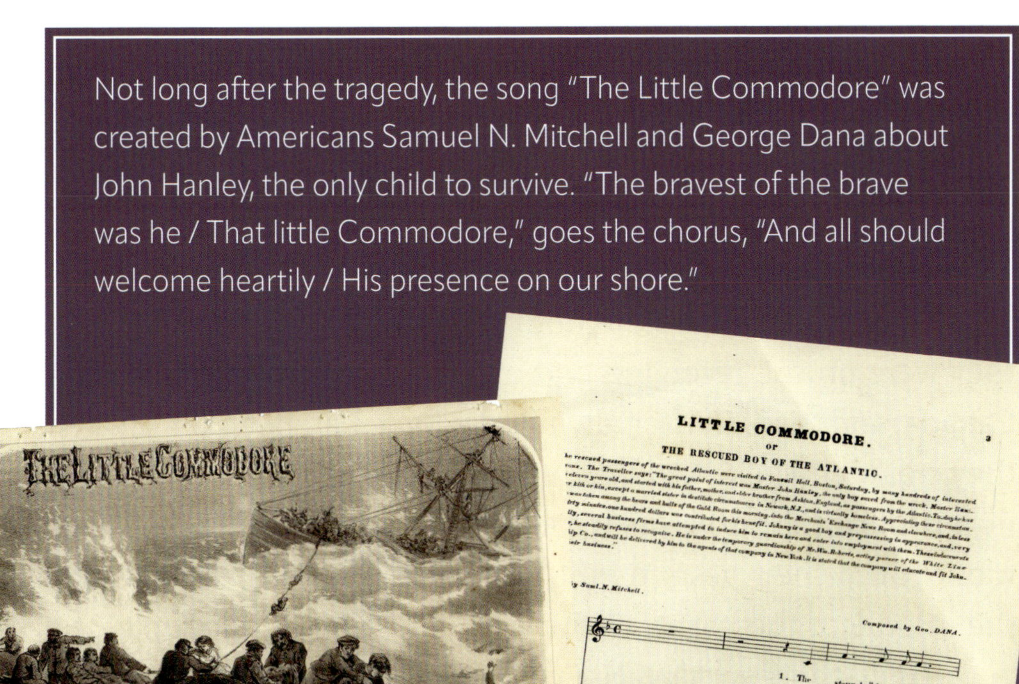

A local haberdasher (someone who sold men's clothing) wanted to do something nice for him, for example, so he brought John to his store and dressed him properly from head to toe for free. Photographers then brought John to their studios and took his portrait, selling copies to raise money for him. Haligonians did what they could for John and many even offered to adopt him into their families. But it felt like some people's interest was also tinged with morbid curiosity: People paid quite a bit of money for his picture as a strange souvenir of the events, and John even got an offer to travel with the circus.

The other survivors were not fussed over quite so much, but they were on the receiving end of generosity in Halifax, across Canada, and the US. After all, many people had been poor when they boarded the SS *Atlantic* in Liverpool or Queenstown, but now a lot of the survivors were penniless. Those who had sewn money into their vests might not have been wearing them in the middle of the night, or the vests had ripped as people desperately tried to survive. Now the money was at the bottom of the sea or lost to its owners forever.

Local shipping companies supplied survivors with what they needed. Captain Williams and saloon-class passengers stayed in the pricey Halifax Hotel, while Chief Engineer John Foxley and other engineers stayed at the less fancy Acadian Hotel. Other crew and passengers were put up at rooming houses and hotels all over the city. One survivor spent a week in hospital in Halifax before he was fit to travel, but most left Halifax quickly, eager to leave the tragedy behind.

On April 3, two hundred passengers continued toward the United States on **steamers** that then connected to trains. They arrived in Boston on April 5 and had a short visit, including meeting the mayor. Bostonians came to see the survivors and raised $100 for John Hanley. Newspapers in Halifax and Boston and New York would end up raising $21,000 in today's money between April 4 and May 15 for the survivors.

Most of the passengers continued to New York City for immigration processing at Castle Garden, where a huge and emotional crowd had been waiting since before dawn. The survivors had a big dinner before boarding yet another steamer to go to the Erie Railroad depot and board trains for their final destinations.

But John Hanley didn't board that steamer: His sisters were at Castle Garden waiting and when he was brought in, his sister Brigid grabbed him in a tight hug, filled with relief, joy, and also grief for the loss of their parents and brother, Michael. People watching the reunion were in tears. But John hadn't seen his sisters in years, since they'd immigrated ahead of the rest of the family, living and working in Newark, New Jersey. Without the easy ways to communicate we have today, the siblings may have felt like strangers.

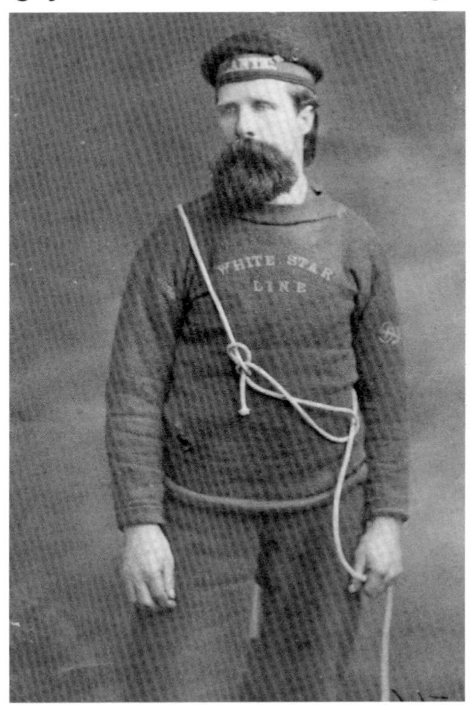

John Speakman, a quartermaster on board the SS Atlantic, *was the first person who managed to swim with a rope from the wreck to the rock in the dark, freezing cold water. When he later arrived home in his village of Crowthorne, England, they gave him a hero's welcome. The village was draped in flags and banners and they celebrated him with a big party.* (NOTMAN STUDIO NOVA SCOTIA ARCHIVES ACCESSION NO. 1983-310 #90095)

Back in Nova Scotia, government and church officials and local people were trying to figure out what to do with the bodies of the disaster victims, people like John Hanley's brother and parents.

At first, victims of the wreck were taken to a spot by a peaceful lagoon between Ryans and Norris Islands, quiet water that boats could get to easily. There was an unused building where the remains could be kept, and space for coffins to be unloaded there as well. That spot became known as the Hill of Death.

Edmund Ryan then worked to document the bodies and try to identify them—by name, nationality, or at the very least by religion so they could be buried in the correct cemetery by a religious official of the right faith. But since many were in nightclothes and hadn't had time to grab anything, often the best they could do was offer a rough description of their age, gender, hair, and any identifying features or objects. Captain Williams, Third Officer Brady, and other crew members also went back to the wreck site to help Edmund Ryan with documenting and identifying human remains.

Many of the twenty-one passengers in saloon class who'd died would be shipped to the United States at the expense of the families or claimed by relatives. Some of those passengers found their final resting place in Halifax: The teenaged Lillian and her mother were buried in Camp Hill Cemetery. Two officers—Second Officer Henry Metcalfe and twenty-three-year-old purser Ambrose Worthington—were also buried in that cemetery.

That left over five hundred bodies that would likely not be claimed, including John Hanley's brother and parents. Even if they had family in North America, most could not afford the trip to Halifax or to have their loved ones' remains shipped home. The Nova Scotia provincial government and the Canadian federal government approved money to pay for burials, and Rev. William Ancient offered space behind St. Paul's Church in Terence Bay—three miles (about five kilometres) from the wreck site by boat—for Protestant victims. As a matter of course, any Jewish people, Muslims, and atheists on board were buried with Protestants as well. Rev. Martin Maas, the Roman Catholic priest at Upper Prospect, spoke up, saying the roughly 250 Catholics could be buried in Lower Prospect alongside what is now called the Star of the Sea Cemetery.

A crew of gravediggers was sent to Terence Bay along with wood for coffins, as well as roughly two hundred coffins that had been quickly constructed in Halifax. If the remains could be identified, someone like Edmund Ryan would write the person's name and place of origin on the outside of the coffin in red chalk.

At the beginning, Ancient and Maas held group burials daily. Coffins were brought over to the site behind St. Paul's Church from the Hill of Death by boat through a narrow channel called Ryans Gut, past the village of Lower Prospect, and along the coast to Tennant Point, where a lighthouse stands today. Rev. Ancient was often on the boat, helping lift coffins, supervising the digging of graves, and covering the coffins properly with dirt.

*There were 277 victims of the wreck buried in the Protestant mass grave in Terence Bay over fifteen burial services. Here Reverend William Ancient, who was involved in the rescue of two survivors from the ship, presides over a funeral service. (*W. CHASE, PUBLIC DOMAIN, VIA NOVA SCOTIA ARCHIVES SHIPS: ATLANTIC / NEGATIVE: N-0719*)*

On April 6, they began filling a long trench dug behind St. Paul's Church with the first 65 bodies. Sometimes they stacked coffins three or four deep. Three days later they buried another 91. For almost three months the burials continued. By June 20, Rev. Ancient and the communities had laid 276 victims of the SS *Atlantic* sinking to rest. Ten days later, a final body was buried at the site, bringing the total there to 277.

A few victims were buried on beaches miles from the wreck site, near where they were found by fishermen or other sailors. One passenger was recovered in Lunenburg, forty miles (sixty-four kilometres) away. In July, Rev. Maas buried the last bodies recovered from the ship, those of a man, woman, and child, in the Catholic cemetery. But there are still many to this day in a watery grave off the shore of Lower Prospect.

The loss of life was terrible, and the toll on survivors and rescuers was huge, but everyone agreed on one thing: The SS *Atlantic* was lucky to have wrecked where there were families who could care for survivors, and brave souls who risked their lives to rescue them. Loved ones from across the ocean and around the world were also grateful to the people of Nova Scotia for treating their deceased family members with as much care as possible. These were silver linings to a heartbreaking tragedy.

Chapter 5

SALVAGE AND BURIALS

During those early days after the shipwreck, telegrams flew back and forth to London and New York as well as Ottawa, the capital of the young nation of Canada. Governments, companies, and newspapers in different places debated: What's the best way to care for the dead and **salvage** the cargo?

Divers and agents were dispatched from New York to work on the wreck, but the site was chaos. And it would get worse before it got better. Starting April 7 a daily shuttle service aboard a steamer called the *Unicorn* started up between Halifax and the wreck site for two dollars per person. Some Haligonians took the day off classes or work to board the *Unicorn* and visit where the SS *Atlantic* had come to grief. People who lived in the nearby communities were suddenly hosting relatives from all over who wanted to see things first-hand. Some show-offs even clambered onto the starboard side of the SS *Atlantic* that was exposed at low tide, and walked around. And, of course, relatives of the victims began arriving looking for their loved ones, along with journalists reporting on this international disaster. Sometimes there were eighty boats at once around the wreck and six or seven hundred people at the site.

Customs officers tried to stop the ship's cargo and individuals' possessions from being stolen, but, as Bob Chaulk writes,

*Many official and unofficial salvagers worked the site in the days, weeks, and months after the wreck to obtain the valuable cargo, lumber, and personal effects of passengers. (*W.R. MACASKILL NOVA SCOTIA ARCHIVES 1987-453 NUMBER 3249*)*

the unwritten law along most seacoasts is that once survivors are rescued, "the ship and anything aboard is fair game." The actual law of the sea, however, is that "As long as the ship is not abandoned…then the ship and its contents remain the property of the owners." So when a person ran into the woods after having stolen a painting, Edmund Ryan, a fisherman and **Justice of the Peace** who'd helped rescue so many the night of the wreck, followed the thief, got the painting back, and gave it to the customs officer.

There were grey areas, though, around items that weren't claimed by any passengers or the White Star Line, like valuable goods **smuggled** aboard the SS *Atlantic*. Those could be auctioned off or used locally, and they were illegal to begin with. And would the White Star Line actually want the lumber floating around that would be so useful to local fishermen? Probably not, but it belonged to the insurance company, and technically people could be charged with stealing and smuggling. The insurance company had a lot at stake and was not going to look the other way. After all, the more cargo they recovered, the less they would have to pay out to the White Star Line. A fisherman was arrested, tried, and found guilty of stealing for scavenging luggage and other goods—but was let off with a fine. He was made an example of to try to stop others, but most agreed he shouldn't have been arrested. And technically the personal effects of dead passengers didn't belong to the White Star Line and they weren't protected by salvage laws.

The money sewn into clothes still on the bodies floating around could certainly tempt people. Newspapers accused fishermen and people from the crowds who came afterward of robbing from the bodies. Some members of the crew and stowaways were even accused of cutting off fingers from bodies to get rings. But Captain Williams inspected remains and didn't see any evidence of that. Even so, author Greg Cochkanoff writes, "An active trade developed in curiosities from the wreck as items were bought and sold along the shore and on the streets of Halifax."

Official and unofficial salvagers used long-handled gaffs and grappling hooks to grab things from the sea, and some used glass-bottomed buckets to look into the crystal-clear water. Edmund Ryan in particular helped document and deliver valuables; by April 10, $6,000 in cash and jewellery had been collected and turned over—more than $150,000 in today's dollars.

The White Star Line's insurance company employed Halifax wrecker John Sheridan and a crew of sixty-five people, including ten divers. As Bob Chaulk writes, they each wore "a canvas suit with a helmet containing tiny windows on the sides and front. On the surface, two men in a boat cranked a manual pump that pushed air down a hose and into the diver's helmet and suit." They were still seventy years away from the scuba technology we are more familiar with today, but they managed.

According to newspaper reports at the time, the salvagers and divers who entered the wreck to get at the cargo said it was a "horrid sight" and called the compartments "chambers of death." When reports came out that the White Star Line hadn't budgeted anything for the divers to recover human remains and were saying that "bodies [were] getting in the way of the job," people, especially relatives, understandably complained. The company was finally shamed into paying to have the bodies recovered—the equivalent of about $1,300 in today's dollars each for the more complex, dangerous, and time-consuming job of recovering saloon class from their cabins, and $500 each for the steerage passengers, who were easier to access.

Because of the way it was lying, though, it was hard to get at the whole ship for salvage and recovery. On April 29, the

Coast Wrecking Company detonated three large explosives. It created a huge blast and pieces of twisted iron apparently flew up into the sky. The deck disconnected from the hull and there were pieces of the ship floating all over the water. It was traumatic for the family members still waiting for the bodies of their loved ones and a man on the shore searching for his still-missing wife wept openly. Then on April 30 the company detonated three more explosions, which blew the upper side of the wreck open. More cargo and bodies dislodged. As bad weather blew in, much of the cargo was swept out to sea.

Local fishermen and their families watched this salvage operation over the following days and weeks. Small schooners would anchor above the wreck and then bring loads to Halifax, where the slightly damaged goods could be auctioned off—luxuries like black silk, pottery, and fancy stockings. But also big items, like a horse-drawn carriage called a phaeton that's still in the collection of Sherbrooke Village, a living museum in Nova Scotia.

They began to wonder: Everyone else involved in the ship's crew and salvage operation was getting paid for their troubles, so why not them? The lawyers representing the fishermen against the White Star Line's insurance company argued the local families had given everything they had to the survivors and were in dire straits. They'd received a bit of aid after the disaster, but had seen others showered with gifts, medals, and money. The three crewmen who got the first rope to the rock, for example—Brady, Speakman, and Owens—all received gold watches, as had Fourth Officer Brown. Brady's was worth $500, about $10,000 in today's dollars!

Survivors did try to raise money and give thanks to the fishermen and their families. A group in Chicago also raised money and sent Sarah Jane O'Reilly a gold locket and chain with twenty pounds sterling. Kate and Agatha O'Brien—two local women who helped care for the survivors—were also gifted lockets and ten pounds. But Rev. William Ancient got a lavish gold pocket watch with an inscription and engraving of the *Atlantic* and $500 from the Canadian government. Together that was like getting $15,000 in today's dollars. Also, Rev. Ancient was honoured by the federal government in front of an audience at the provincial legislature, while Sarah Jane had her reward simply dropped off at her house by Rev. Ancient.

Yes, Rev. Ancient had participated in the rescue, but the stories in newspapers across the country, being preached in churches, and even announced in Canadian parliament were exaggerated. Even though Rev. Ancient had carried out an amazing rescue of two men, it was still just two men. The people of Lower and Upper Prospect had rescued nearly four hundred. Why did the newspapers latch on to Rev. Ancient so much? Likely for many reasons: He was a great public speaker, he had been in the British Navy, and he was educated and English. Meanwhile, the fishermen and their families near the wreck site were working-class and Irish. At that time, there was **prejudice** against the Irish, and they were often looked down upon by the English in Great Britain as well as North America.

The fishermen only wanted to have their expenses covered and to receive fair compensation for their time and effort. Especially when the White Star Line and its insurance company were being so stingy with them, the survivors' families, and the care of the dead. The fishermen brought their case to a special naval court called the vice-admiralty court, and their lawyer raised the promises made by Captain Williams of $500 per load of people—again, about $10,000 in today's dollars. Even if they were promises made in desperation and Williams didn't have the authority to make them, witnesses had heard and believed him.

*Rev. William Ancient was the Protestant minister in Terence Bay at the time of the wreck. He got a lot of attention for his actions rescuing the last two men on the ship, while the courageous fishermen and their compassionate family members who came to the aid of hundreds of survivors were often overlooked. (*NOTMAN STUDIO NOVA SCOTIA ARCHIVES ACCESSION NO. 1983-310 #90088 / NEGATIVE: N-6280*)*

Some victims' families brought lawsuits against the White Star Line as well. With the loss of the ship, its cargo, and the company's reputation, the survival of the company was at stake. Perhaps that's why the insurance company's lawyer said the fishermen had been stealing from the wreck and bodies. The White Star Line also changed its earlier story to say the captain and crew did most of the rescuing—even though the owner of the White Star Line had originally said the fishermen saved the survivors.

In the end, the Canadian Government sent $3,000 to cover the burials, coffins, and rewards to be bestowed "on deserving individuals." A total of $736.60 went to the fishermen named in the lawsuit and $823.40 was distributed to others in the three communities who helped the survivors. Then the next year the vice-admiralty court gave between $30 and $150 per person, depending on various factors. Most received $60 or $100.

A few weeks after the disaster, a big storm finally sank what was left of the SS *Atlantic,* and much of the salvage operations stopped. But there were still many questions to be answered.

Chapter 6

"A GRAVE ERROR"

On April 5, the first day the divers could get into the water at the wreck site, an inquiry began in Halifax to try to figure out what had gone so wrong as well as who was to blame. A committee of three local officials connected to shipping questioned twenty-three crew and passengers from the SS *Atlantic* as well as some expert witnesses. How could this modern ship in perfect condition, with well-qualified officers from the world's top seafaring nation, up-to-date naval charts, and approaching a well-known harbour, have ended up wrecking so far off course?

It was true that weather changed often and quickly, and could be different over short distances. And yes, in 1873 shipwrecks were a relatively common occurrence. But this was the largest transatlantic passenger ship disaster in the North Atlantic to date, with around 550 men, women, and children dead. People around the English-speaking world were outraged. There were even calls in England to have Captain Williams charged with murder.

At the investigation, First Officer John Firth declared, "The captain exercised all the care and caution necessary. During the twenty-seven years that I have followed the sea, I have not seen a better captain."

But was that actually true?

Captain Williams was already walking with a limp and using a cane after being seriously injured aboard a ship that got caught out in a hurricane the year before. He had spent months in hospital recovering from a broken leg and ribs among other injuries. He couldn't get around the ship to supervise as much as usual, and the work of a ship's captain at the time was very physically demanding. Most people would struggle with the irregular sleep, being outdoors in all kinds of weather, being on your feet for hours at a time on an unsteady and unreliable floor, and constantly climbing up and down stairs. Captain Williams was also known to say that since his accident, the cold and being in dark spaces—like where the coal was stored—were harder for him.

Then a top newspaper, *The New York Times*, dug into Captain Williams's past and discovered he'd likely been fired from another company for drinking too much alcohol while on duty. The White Star Line had given him a job on the understanding he'd changed his ways, though, and the newspaper reported, "He was bright, active and was soon promoted rapidly."

But Williams had apparently not said anything about the strong currents to his officers or mentioned that he had instructed the steward to bring him hot chocolate and wake him up. He had made an error in navigation and put the ship off course, and his lying down to sleep, even fully clothed, made the rest of the crew think it was a routine voyage, even though Halifax Harbour was unknown to most on board.

Captain Williams expressed deep remorse in interviews with newspapers and talked about what he should have done differently. At the inquiry, Captain Williams read a prepared statement. In it, he said, "The one thing I regret is that I was too sure of my course." Still, he maintained, the officers should have been able to see things and reversed the engines in time. But as he continued, he broke down crying: "What more can I suffer? If it were not for my wife and three little children at home, I should never have been here; I'd have stuck to that vessel till the last and gone down with her."

The inquiry finished in Halifax on April 18, 1873. After listening to two weeks of testimony and reading 120 pages of transcripts, the inquiry board came to some conclusions about the "grave errors" that took place. First, the officers on duty should have checked how deep the water was more often. According to them, this was the worst error. But they also reprimanded Captain Williams for leaving the bridge that night and Fourth Officer Brown for not calling the captain earlier. Brown lost his certificate for four months while Captain Williams was found to be responsible for the wreck and lost his certificate for two years. The fact he behaved so admirably during the disaster and the inquiry helped his case, though, and he did not lose it permanently.

The inquiry report makes no mention of Henry Metcalfe, the twenty-eight-year-old Second Officer who was in charge of the ship at the time of the wreck. Author Greg Cochkanoff says this was probably "out of respect for his death and his inability to defend himself." More recently, author Bob Chaulk researched the facts of officer Metcalfe's life and untimely death: Chaulk discovered Metcalfe was cousin to White Star Line owner Thomas Ismay, so might have been hired because of the family connection and not his skill. After all, Metcalfe had a few black marks on his record. A few years earlier, he was asleep on the job while in command of a ship that ran into a French barque off the coast of Brazil. There were crew injuries and deaths, and quite a few deserted the ship. He wasn't allowed to work as a first mate on a ship for a year as punishment. When that time was up, he went back to work aboard various ships in his cousin's company, eventually ending up on the SS *Atlantic*, promoted above a more knowledgeable and experienced sailor, Cornelius Lawrence Brady. The night of the SS *Atlantic* disaster, Chaulk says Officer Metcalfe should have woken the captain up at 3 A.M. when no one had spotted Sambro Light—or if he wasn't sure of things. Metcalfe certainly should not have sent away the steward with the hot cocoa, because why else would a steward bring a drink to a captain at 3 A.M. unless the captain had specifically ordered it?

Finally, and most damaging for the company, the inquiry said the White Star Line did not have enough coal on board, which led Captain Williams to divert to Halifax in the first place.

The victims' loved ones were unhappy with the findings and called for further digging. T. H. Ismay and the White Star Line also wanted another hearing, because they wanted to prove there had been enough coal on board and it was the captain's error that led to the disaster. That way, people would still sail on the company's ships and the White Star Line would keep their big money-making mail contracts.

The next investigation began May 10 in Liverpool, England, from where the SS *Atlantic* had departed just over a month earlier. The Board of Trade called nineteen witnesses, including local experts on shipping and coal, to grill them about the ship's working conditions and if there had been enough coal before the *Atlantic* left England. Those experts stated that everything was ship-shape: from the amount and quality of food and water, to the cleanliness of the bunks, to the operating of boilers. The certificates of the instruments were up to date, and the lifeboats, life preservers, and oars were all present, sufficient, and in good working order.

Fated for calamity?

Apparently one of the worst storms of the season lay on the SS *Atlantic*'s planned route to New York City. If they hadn't diverted to Halifax, they would have gone smack into it. Maybe the SS *Atlantic* was always doomed.

The Board of Trade in England was satisfied with everything except the coal question. It found, once again, that the SS *Atlantic* was short and needed to divert to Halifax. Ismay complained and the inquiry started up again two weeks later just to focus on the coal situation. Ismay and his company brought every expert they could think of to support their case: engineers, other ship owners, past captains, and ship builders. Finally, on June 11 the judgement came down: The ship was definitely short of coal partway through the journey when it should not have been. If this was the case, though, it would look really bad not only for the company but for the English authorities who had signed off that the SS *Atlantic* was fit to sail. So the Board of Trade sifted once more through all the materials from the inquiries and investigations. That careful checking led them to a different conclusion: There had, in fact, been enough coal.

The problem was that the captain had been led to believe there wasn't enough.

And why was that? In the end, they found holes in Chief Engineer John Foxley's stories—contradictions in terms of how much coal was on board and what he'd told his captain. The engineers were supposed to count each basket to tally how much had been used and how much was left. But Foxley hadn't been keeping proper track of the baskets of coal—how much they could carry and how many loads were being burned. Foxley had, in fact, been "guesstimating" and lying to the captain about it and then had changed his story during the inquiry and afterward publicly in the press. The captain also didn't follow the rules properly, as he was supposed to get detailed reports from the chief engineer and double-check the coal supply himself. He likely skipped this because of how physically hard it was to go into the cold, dark space where the coal was stored.

There had, in fact, been enough coal to last the voyage to New York, and no need to divert to Halifax and be anywhere near the rocky shores of Nova Scotia in the early morning hours of April 1, 1873.

Bob Chaulk says this might be why Foxley left the SS *Atlantic* along with Brady and some others right after the wreck to hike into Halifax. While Brady had an important mission to relay information to the company from Halifax, Foxley should have stayed behind to help protect the ship from salvagers. Instead, he left, possibly out of shame or embarrassment, and not wanting to see the consequence of his actions.

In the end, another of Captain Williams's fatal errors was trusting Chief Engineer Foxley too much.

Captain Williams, Chief Engineer Foxley, and others on board the SS *Atlantic* had to live with the knowledge of their mistakes for the rest of their lives. In the case of Captain Williams, he only went to sea one more time after the disaster, in late 1874, as third officer on a small cargo steamer to India. After that he and his wife bought a hotel in England and ran it for many years, raising their six children. His wife never wanted anyone to speak of the SS *Atlantic*, and their great-grandson later wrote, "I had a sense that there was some dark secret no one was sharing."

Chapter 7

MEMORIES

The White Star Line—and the British press generally—also seemed to avoid the topic of the SS *Atlantic* as much as possible, and tried to erase the tragedy in the coming weeks and months. Since the disaster was caused by human error, it was a huge embarrassment to the proud seafaring nation *and* the shipping company. Even writers doing profiles of the White Star Line's history in the years following the disaster left out the story of the SS *Atlantic*—actually removing its name completely from ads and articles. They wanted to focus on success and safety and ignore mistakes and tragedies.

The passengers could not forget the wreck, though. Some of the survivors were physically and emotionally scarred from the experience, especially those who lost loved ones. Twelve-year-old John Hanley's brother and parents had died, and he'd gone through an incredibly scary time on the ship. Even though he survived and went to live with his sisters in Newark, New Jersey, all of that weighed heavily on him. There were no grief counsellors or therapists like today, and people struggled with what we might now call post-traumatic stress disorder (PTSD) or survivor's guilt (for those on the ship). Likely because of this,

John Hanley lived a short and troubled life, dying at the age of thirty-five.

The people in Terence Bay, Lower Prospect, and Upper Prospect also had their lives completely turned upside down, and the terrors of the early morning hours of April 1 continued to haunt the locals' nightmares and plague their memories. Older people in the community apparently told their stories to reporters and visitors, bursting into tears each time they recounted the events. A journalist for the *New-York Tribune* visited Michael Clancy in his home and wrote about how when he described "the haggard, frenzied, half-crazed people who crowded into his house, the tears ran down his face in streams." With all this pain and suffering swirling, ghost stories took root in the area about the wreck. A couple of years later, one citizen of Upper Prospect was even admitted to a psychiatric care facility, the Nova Scotia Hospital for the Insane as it was then known, after having delusions about the *Atlantic* and saying he was tormented by the devil.

But life went on, and the newspapers' interest in the wreck waned after a month. There were short updates on the salvage and burials and recoveries, but the wreck site was now submerged, and with the inquiries and salvage operations over, there weren't any breaking news stories.

Memories of the wreck also began to fade over time. Wooden markers were erected at the time of the burials, but these didn't last very long in the elements. At the Protestant and Catholic cemeteries where the mass graves had been created, there were no headstones with people's birthplaces, dates, or names like you might typically find. When Michael Clancy and Edmund Ryan and other fishermen from the area central to the rescue died in the 1890s—about twenty years after the wreck—burial sites had already begun to deteriorate. This was for several reasons: People were busy surviving, those buried did not have local family members, and the burial sites were challenging to get to by foot or boat.

The 1905 memorial at the Protestant mass grave site still stands today. (DANIELLE METCALFE-CHENAIL)

Then, in 1905, decades after the shipwreck, Rev. A. F. Dentith, from St. Paul's Church in Terence Bay—Rev. Ancient's old church—wrote to the White Star Line about the state of the graves and getting a permanent marker on the site. The company sent funds and Rev. Dentith, along with several dignitaries and religious officials, unveiled a new eight-foot-tall granite monument on December 7, 1905. The now sixty-nine-year-old Rev. Ancient attended and gave a speech to the assembled crowd. A few months later, on the anniversary of the shipwreck, *The Halifax Herald* published a letter from Sarah Jane O'Reilly, who had helped so many the night of the disaster. She wanted to tell the story from her perspective and that of the people of Prospect, which was different from what Rev. Ancient shared.

Interest in the SS *Atlantic* faded in and out over the coming years. The Atlantic Memorial Elementary School in Shad Bay was built and named in 1959 in an attempt to remember the disaster. But most people still don't know it's connected to the shipwreck. They think it's about the Atlantic Ocean and people from the area lost at sea or in the two World Wars, perhaps.

By 1969 the Protestant gravesite in Terence Bay was just a tangle of brambles and bushes. *The Halifax Herald* reported that people even used the 1906 memorial for target practice, so it was covered in black bullet marks. At that point, a representative for Terence Bay asked: "The graves of the *Titanic* victims buried in Fairview Cemetery in Halifax are kept up, so why not the graves of the *Atlantic*?"

In 1980 local people called a town meeting, raised funds, and went to work clearing a path from the new St. Paul's Cemetery through the woods to the monument and common Protestant grave. They fixed up the monument, re-detailed the inscription, and made a new base to surround it. From there, they cleared the historic pioneer cemetery and created a path to the ruins of the old St. Paul's Church that had burned down decades earlier. The group beautified the surrounding area and made it accessible so people could come spend time picnicking and paying their respects. During this time, work was also done on the Star of the Sea Cemetery and a monument was erected to the 250 Roman Catholic victims. Finally, a new plaque was placed on Sarah Jane O'Reilly's grave.

Approximately 250 Roman Catholic victims of the wreck are buried alongside the Star of the Sea Cemetery in Lower Prospect. (DANIELLE METCALFE-CHENAIL)

By the 1990s, people in the area noticed **erosion** clawing away the shoreline and exposing gravesites at the Protestant site. One person recalled that when she was thirteen years old she'd been playing there—even though her parents had told her to stay away—and noticed what was left of a woman's lace-up boot and the bones of a human hand. So the community brought in heavy equipment to overhaul the shore and bank below the gravesite, creating a stone barrier against the crashing ocean waves.

In 1995, one of the first visitors to the restored site was a relative of John Hanley, the twelve-year-old boy who had survived the wreck. When this relative saw a picture of John at the heritage centre she started to cry. "He looked just like my Uncle Bill," she said.

These positive experiences encouraged local citizens to create the SS *Atlantic* Memorial Committee in the late 1990s to preserve the story of the disaster and the final resting place of the victims. They raised money to build the SS *Atlantic* Heritage Park and Interpretation Centre, which opened in 2002. Bob Chaulk became committed to correcting the exaggerations and misinformation that circulated after the wreck, confusing fact and fiction. At the time of the wreck, he says, there were hundreds of experiences, opinions, and prejudices that coloured the stories that were circulated. There wasn't much photography at the time, and artistic

A dedicated group of staff and volunteers share the story of the SS Atlantic *at the Heritage Park and Interpretation Centre. The centre is open in the summer months and visitors are welcome to hike the trail and boardwalk any time of year.* (DANIELLE METCALFE-CHENAIL)

imaginings appeared in newspapers that got stuck in people's minds. "After a century and a half of telling and retelling the story," he writes in his book *Atlantic's Last Stop*, "too many people filled the gaps with errors, guesses, lies, and assumptions."

The next step was to contact Dr. Jonathan Fowler at St. Mary's University in 2019. Dr. Fowler teaches an advanced archaeology course, and he and his students arrived with their instruments in the fall of 2019 and went to work using three different methods. "We more or less outlined the mass grave. We presented our results to the community, that the grave actually goes outside

Dr. Jonathan Fowler and some of his archaeology students from Saint Mary's University in Halifax have been doing fieldwork at the Protestant mass grave. They hope to return to help with the Catholic one as well. (JONATHAN FOWLER)

the roped-off area you see at the site." Then COVID happened, and things got shut down.

But interest continued to rise in the SS *Atlantic*, especially as American archaeologist and documentary filmmaker Tom Lynskey began posting his videos about the disaster to his YouTube channel, *Part-Time Explorer*. Lynskey had come across the story while visiting Halifax, and became interested in learning all he could about the wreck, what caused it, and the final resting places of a few passengers who had seemingly disappeared. As of July 2025, there were over 5 million views of his SS *Atlantic* videos.

From that work, Wisconsin historian Frank Jastrzembski became interested in Rev. William Ancient's grave at St. John's Cemetery in Halifax, near 121 *Titanic* victims. Jastrzembski was surprised to find the site unmarked in 2020, so he raised money and had a tombstone placed that says: "Four volunteers led by Ancient rescued the last survivors of the SS *Atlantic*."

In 2023, the SS *Atlantic* Heritage Park and Interpretation Centre commemorated the 150th anniversary of the wreck with community activities such as a quilt and new memorials in Lower and Upper Prospect, as well as school activities that saw Atlantic Memorial Elementary School students make flags that were flown on the famous *Bluenose II* schooner.

The work is not quite done, and may never be. "We're still interested in that site and story and in touch with community members," Dr. Fowler says. "We'd like to return to the area and, once we ID high potential sites [for the Catholic mass grave], we'd like to use dogs, which can discover human remains after many centuries. We can also use Ground Penetrating Radar (GPR) again, electromagnetic induction, and LIDAR (Light Detection and Ranging). Every instrument sees the world in a slightly different way. Put all that data together and we will have a holistic picture."

*The 150th anniversary memorials in Upper and Lower Prospect. They honour the courage and compassion of the communities that helped so many strangers. (*DANIELLE METCALFE-CHENAIL)

Epilogue

You can still visit the SS *Atlantic* Heritage Park and Interpretation Centre. If you enter the small white building filled with objects and stories from the ship, bring your curiosity and staff will be more than happy to answer your questions. Then wander the seaside trail from the old church ruins to the Protestant mass gravesite so you can pay your respects to those who lost their lives, honour the brave rescuers, and learn from the storyboards as seagulls screech and waves rush the shore.

You can't see the wreck from there, though, not even with binoculars. The site is actually three miles (around five kilometres) away and can only be accessed by boat or air. You can go on Google Maps, though, and look at Ryans Island and beyond, to Golden Rule Rock, imagining the path the brave rescuers took to the SS *Atlantic*. Or, if you put on your scuba gear and descend into the frigid water offshore, you'll find a peaceful place full of seaweed and kelp waving in the currents. There's no recognizable shipwreck underwater like you might see in a movie; the salvage process at the time and winter storms since have ground away whatever was left. But if you can get there on a rare day when the water is clear and not too rough, you might spot broken china, coins, bottles, and bits of jewellery in among the starfish, sea urchins, lobsters, and crabs.

You might even be able to contribute to what we know about the SS *Atlantic*, and be part of that growing history, because there are still stories to be told, mysteries to be solved, and lessons to be learned from this terrifying disaster all those years ago—and from the courageous and compassionate people who saved the lives of so many.

Scuba diving

Since the 1970s, when scuba diving became more accessible to average people, the SS *Atlantic* has been a popular site. It's close to shore and not too deep, so easier to access. It's still a tough site to dive because of strong winds that churn up the sea, and not much of the ship is recognizable anymore after being pummelled by 150 years of storms. In this picture, Bob Chaulk is eighty feet down examining the remains of tubes from the ship's boilers. Even when conditions are good, the diving can be challenging with rough seas, strong currents, and poor visibility. Over the years divers have found things like worn toothbrushes, parts of lice combs, and even gold coins. The odd piece of costume jewellery, broken china, coins, or a bent spoon or fork still turn up every now and then.

From the 1970s onward, scuba divers visited the wreck site. (BOB SEMPLE)

Acknowledgements

Thank you to Whitney Moran and the Nimbus team for getting excited at the idea for this book, and to Claire Bennet for shepherding the project along and being such a great support. Penelope Jackson—thank you for your keen eye and clarifying questions. Bee Stanton—you have outdone yourself with the graphic design!

A big thanks to Mercedes Peters, Bob Chaulk, and Lynette Richards, who reviewed the manuscript, and to Frank Jastrzembski and Dr. Jonathan Fowler for fascinating correspondence and conversation. Melony Boutilier helped me with an important ocean science question at the last minute. Any errors that remain are entirely on me!

Deep appreciation to my literary agent, Elizabeth Copps, for helping me with the admin side of things and being part of my cheering section. My writing community has been so key to my journey (too many to name!) and I am immensely grateful for the quiet time I spent working at Jampolis Cottage in Avonport, Nova Scotia, and Hedgebrook Farm on Whidby Island, Washington State.

Finally, I'm especially grateful to my husband and kids, who spent a lot of time walking the SS *Atlantic* heritage site with me and listening as I researched and wrote this book. They help me be more compassionate and courageous every day!

Want to Learn More?

Books

Chaulk, Bob. *Atlantic's Last Stop.* (Nimbus Publishing, 2021).

Cochkanoff, Greg, and Bob Chaulk. *SS Atlantic: The White Star Line's First Disaster at Sea*. (Goose Lane, 2009).

Fitch, Sheree. *The Gravesavers*. (Puffin Canada, 2005).

Richards, Lynette. *Call Me Bill.* (Conundrum Press, 2022).

Vivier, Carmel. *Shipwrecks off the East Coast* (James Lorimer & Company, 2009).

Websites

SS *Atlantic* Heritage Park and Interpretation Centre: ssatlantic.com

SS *Atlantic* Legacy Art Project: ssatlantic150projects.com

Part-Time Explorer videos on YouTube by Tom Lynskey

Discussion Questions

1. Who do you think was responsible for the wreck of the SS *Atlantic*?

2. What could the crew have done to prevent the disaster?

3. If you'd been on board the SS *Atlantic* or among the rescuers, what would you have done?

4. Why did people at the time have different ideas about what happened with the SS *Atlantic*?

5. Who would you have given medals and rewards to? Why?

6. What do you think of the way Captain Williams acted after the tragedy?

7. Why do you think the *Titanic* shipwreck is so famous and ones like the SS *Atlantic* are less known?

8. Why do we share and remember tragedies like shipwrecks over 100 years later?

Glossary

Ballast: Something heavy that is on a ship to keep it steady and balanced.

Boiler: A machine that makes steam to power and heat the ship.

Bow: The front of the boat.

Bridge: A room or area where the captain and crew control the ship.

Cargo: All the stuff a ship is carrying.

Colonial: Relating to a colony, which is a country or territory under full or partial control by another country, often far away, with settlers from that country claiming the land.

Dory: A simple and light boat used for fishing or rowing near the shore.

Erosion: When water, wind, or weather slowly wears things away.

Haligonian: The name given to someone from Halifax, Nova Scotia.

Helm: The place where you steer a ship or boat.

Hull: The main body of the ship.

Inquiry: When someone asks questions and looks for answers after a ship accident.

Justice of the Peace: A person who helps make sure the law is being followed and can help solve small legal problems.

Knots: Nautical miles per hour.

Mast: A tall pole on a ship that holds up the sails.

Musket: An old-fashioned gun that is long and heavy, and that you had to load with gunpowder and a bullet.

Officer: A person who helps run the ship and gives orders.

Porthole: A small, round window on a ship.

Prejudice: Judging someone—usually in an unfair way—before you really know them.

Ration: The amount and type of food given out to crew.

Rigging: All the ropes and cables on a ship.

Salvage: Saving or recovering something that was lost or in danger.

Seine: A large rowboat used for fishing.

Smuggle: Secretly take something somewhere, usually because it's illegal.

Steamer: A big ship that uses steam power to move.

Stern: The back of a boat.

Stowaway: Someone who sneaks on board a ship without permission.

Tonnage: For ships, this usually means how much space it has inside for carrying cargo.

Index

Discover more books in the Compass Series!

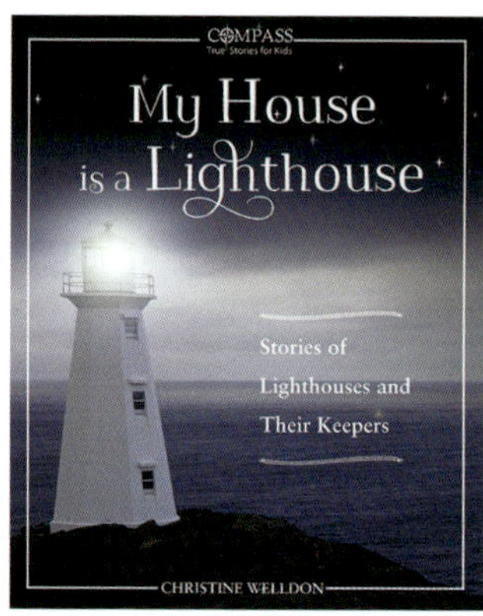

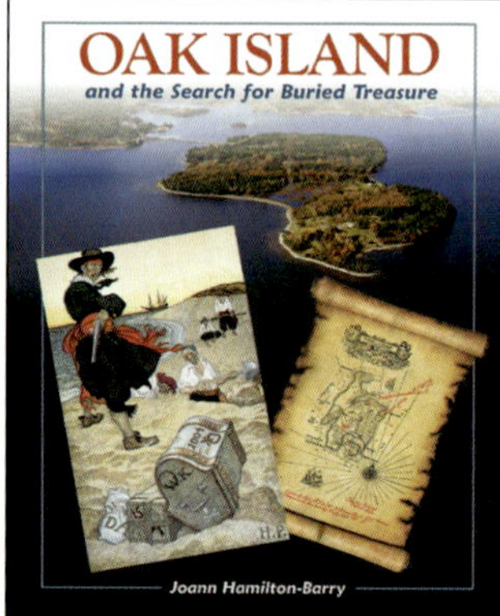

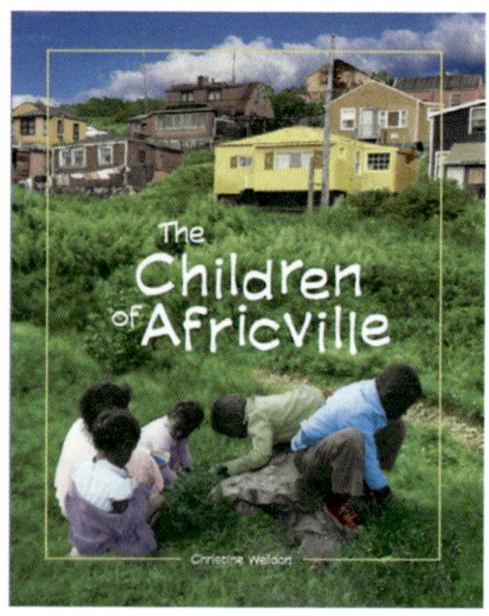

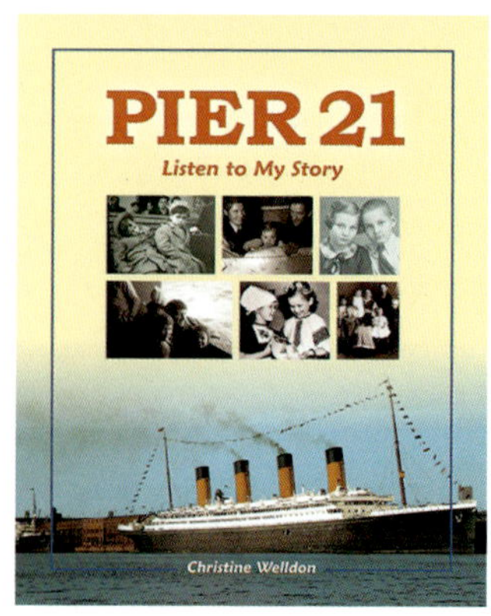

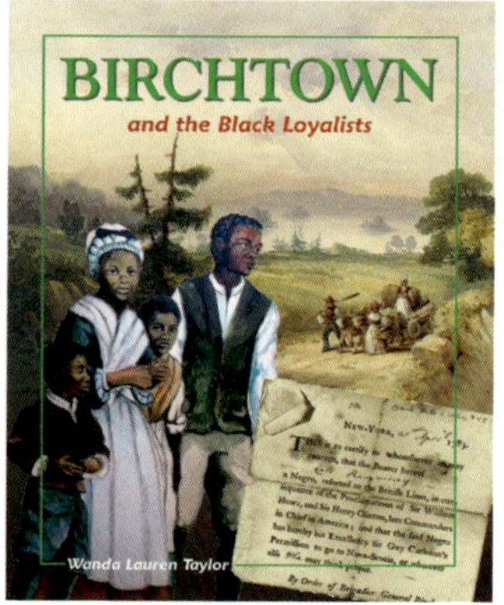